Paragraph and
Topic Sent

A paragraph is a group of sentences that tell about the same subject. Each paragraph is indented at the beginning.

Number your answer sheet from 1 to 4. Read each paragraph. If all the sentences in the paragraph tell about the same subject, write **Yes** next to the number. If some sentences do not belong in the paragraph, write **No** next to the number. Then write the sentence or sentences that do not belong in the paragraph.

1 More than 200 years ago, pirates ruled the seas. At least, that's the way it seemed to poor travelers who tried to sail from one part of the world to another. There were pirates in the Mediterranean, which was a major trading route. There were pirates in the Caribbean, which was a gold and silver shipping route. There were pirates in the China Sea, and there were pirates in the Pacific. Pirates were everywhere.

2 Do you know what a farrier is? Very few people know what that word means. That's because there aren't many farriers around. And those that are around don't call themselves farriers. A few of the fancy ones call themselves hoof mechanics. A hoof mechanic, of course, is a blacksmith. A blacksmith is a person who shoes horses. So a farrier, hoof mechanic, and blacksmith are all the same thing. Horses are very nice animals.

1

3   There is a fish called the mosquitofish.   The fish does not look like a mosquito. It does not buzz like a mosquito. Fish live in salt water or in fresh water. And it does not bite people like a mosquito does. What the mosquitofish does is eat mosquitoes.

4   In 1901, Theodore Roosevelt became President of the United States. One of his goals was to build a canal through Panama to connect the Atlantic and Pacific Oceans. It took 10 years to build the Panama Canal, but the canal cut the Boston to San Francisco trip by 7800 miles. Without the canal, the same trip was 13,000 miles.

EXERCISE **2**

Number your answer sheet from 1 to 5. Read all the sentences below. Write the letters of the five sentences that belong in the same paragraph.

A.   A Dalmatian is a large white dog with black spots.

B.   Dalmatians were bred to be coach dogs.

C.   Coach dogs are dogs that used to run alongside the horses who pulled a coach.

D.   Coaches were very uncomfortable.

E.   Today people don't ride in coaches.

F.   Dalmatians don't chase after coaches anymore, but they do something even more exciting.

G.   Dalmatians get to ride in fire trucks because many fire stations have **Dalmatians** as mascots.

2

EXERCISE 3

Number your answer sheet from 1 to 8. Read all the sentences below. Write the letters of the eight sentences that belong in the same paragraph.

A. If you had a Dalmatian, you could name it spot, of course.

B. You could also name it Spots since it would have more than one spot.

C. If you wanted to be clever, you could name it Spotless.

D. When your friends would ask why you named it Spotless, you could say that it was a clean dog.

E. Friends have a way of asking strange questions.

F. Maybe you could name the dog Polka Dot, or Polka Dots.

G. You could name it Leopard, or even Peppered.

H. Do you enjoy naming animals.?

I. You could name it Dice, or Snake Eyes, or Measles.

J. You could really use your imagination in naming a Dalmatian.

EXERCISE 4

Number your answer sheet from 1 to 6. Read all the sentences below. Write the letters of the six sentences that belong in the same paragraph.

A. Most of the important fruits of the world belong to one of two families.

B. One of the families is the rose family.

C. The fruits that are members of the rose family are the apple, peach, apricot, nectarine, plum, and cherry.

D. The strawberry does not belong to the rose family.

E. Strawberries are my favorite fruit.

F. The second important fruit family is the citrus family.

G. Oranges and tangerines are members of the citrus family.

H. So are lemons, limes, and grapefruits.

I. Bananas are not members of the citrus family.

3

Number your answer sheet from 1 to 5. Read all the sentences below. Write the letters of the five sentences that belong in the same paragraph.

A.   Most everybody has had the hiccups at one time or another.
B.   Many things can cause hiccups.
C.   There are 33 different diseases that can cause hiccups.
D.   Eating spicy food can cause them.
E.   People should avoid spicy food.
F.   Fright can also cause hiccups.
G.   So can eating or drinking too fast.
H.   There are many so-called cures for hiccups.

Each paragraph has a main idea. The main idea tells what the paragraph is about. Turn back to Exercise 1 and read the first paragraph. The main idea of that paragraph is that more than 200 years ago there were pirates on all the seas.

Now read the second paragraph in Exercise 1. The main idea of that paragraph is that a farrier is a blacksmith.

Number your answer sheet from 1 to 7. Read each paragraph. Write a sentence that tells what you think the main idea of each paragraph is.

1   Nobody, not even doctors, know for sure how to cure hiccups. But everybody thinks he or she knows how to cure hiccups. Many people think that if you breathe into a paper bag you will get rid of the hiccups. Some think that if you swallow dry bread you will cure the hiccups. Others say you must drink a glass of water. Some people put vinegar on the tongue, and others try to swallow hot sauce. Sometimes these tricks work, and sometimes they don't.

2   People can change the wildlife in an area through carelessness. In Hawaii, people who had small pet lizards let them escape. The lizards grew to be five feet long in the wild. Now Hawaii has iguana lizards in it. In Montana, some people got tired of taking care of their tropical fish. So they put them into some of Montana's hot springs. Now there are thousands of tropical fish in some of Montana's waters.

3   A setter is a dog that was bred to hunt birds by crouching, or "setting," in front of them. Hunters used to catch birds with the help of setters before there were guns. The dog's master would creep up to the dog with a huge net. The master would then throw the net over the dog and the birds. That is how hunters used to catch birds with the help of a setter.

4   There are three kinds of setters raised today. The one most popular with hunters is the English setter. It is a long-haired white dog with black flecks all over its coat. The one considered the most beautiful is the Irish setter. It has a red coat. The one that fewest people know about is the Gordon setter. It is black with tan markings on its head and chest.

5   Plants in a desert have special features that help them survive the hot, dry weather. Some desert plants have roots that grow down as deep as 175 feet to reach underground water. Others have roots that spread out in a wide circle to collect more water. Still other desert plants store water in their roots, stems and leaves.

6   Blackbeard the pirate had a black beard, long black hair, and black hands and face. The reason he had black hands and a black face was that he never washed. He would use his hands for eating or working or fighting. Then he would wipe them across his face and beard. He never took a bath or cleaned his clothes. He was frightening to look at and frightening to smell.

7   Today blacksmiths shoe horses in two different ways. Western horses and pleasure horses are shod like they always were. The iron shoes are hammered to fit their hooves. But show horses must have special treatment. These horses must jump and take all kinds of fancy steps. When a blacksmith shoes these horses, he must put a padding of leather between the horse's hoof and the iron shoe.

The main idea of a paragraph is usually expressed in a topic sentence. The topic sentence is one sentence which tells what the paragraph is about. It is often, but not always, the first sentence in a paragraph.

Turn back to Exercise 1 and read the first paragraph. The topic sentence is the first sentence: "More than 200 years ago, pirates ruled the seas."

Now read the second paragraph in Exercise 1. The topic sentence is the next-to-last sentence: "So a farrier, hoof mechanic, and blacksmith are all the same thing."

EXERCISE **7**

Number your answer sheet from 1 to 6. Read each paragraph. The line in each paragraph shows where the missing topic sentence should go. Write a topic sentence on your paper for each paragraph. Remember that the topic sentence should tell the main idea of the paragraph. Here are the topic sentences to choose from:

- These two tricks will help you get bubble gum off of your face and clothes.

- The Great Dane was a very powerful dog.

- Pyramids have been built around the world.

- There are many mystery stories for young people.

- Camels are well suited to desert life.

- Some contests are strange.

1 _____. The mystery series about Trixie Belden and her brothers is for young people. So are the books about Frank and Joe Hardy. And so are the books about Nancy Drew. The books about the young detective known as Encyclopedia Brown are also for young people.

2 _____. The pyramids of Egypt, built between 2700 B.C. and 2200 B.C., are the oldest. In Mexico, around A.D. 900 and A.D. 1200, the Castillo pyramid was built at Chichen Itza. America and France have modern-day pyramids. The American pyramid is in Memphis, Tennessee.

3 Many people use ice cubes to help get bubble gum off of their faces, shoes, or clothing. The ice causes the gum to turn hard. Then they can lift the gum right off. Another trick to getting bubble gum off of faces and hands is peanut butter. If you have gum all over your face, rub your face with peanut butter. Then rub the peanut butter off. That will take the gum off, too. _____.

4 _____. One of these strange contests is a bubble gum blowing contest. A bunch of people of all ages stand around chewing bubble gum. Then each person blows the biggest bubble he or she can. The person who blows the biggest bubble without breaking it wins the contest.

5 In the days of the early Greeks and Romans, Great Danes were used to fight lions. A lion weighs three times more than a Great Dane, but often the dog would win the fight. In Germany in ancient times, packs of Great Danes were used to hunt wild boars. Boars were very dangerous animals. But the Great Danes got rid of the boars and made the forest safe for people to walk through. _____.

6 A hump, wide feet, long eyelashes and nostrils that open and close, are all features of camels. Their hump consists of fat cells that store water. Their long eyelashes and closable nostrils keep sand out of their eyes and nose. And a camel's broad feet keep them from sinking in the sand. _____.

EXERCISE 8

Number your answer sheet from 1 to 6. Read each paragraph. Write the topic sentence of the paragraph on your paper.

1 Not all deserts are hot. A desert is any location that lacks available water for plants and animals. This means that the Arctic and Antarctica are deserts, too. The water in these two polar regions is frozen and can't be used by plants and animals. Whether hot or cold, desert environments are harsh regions of the world.

2 People wear masks for many reasons. Halloweeners wear them in order to fool people and get treats. Outlaws wear them so that they won't be recognized. People at parties wear them just for fun. In ancient Greece actors used to wear them to play different parts on the stage. And in ancient China warriors used to wear them in battle to frighten their enemies.

3 Antarctica is the coldest place in the world. The temperature is often cold enough to freeze flesh at -40°F! Wind speed can reach 200 miles an hour. No people live there permanently. The only land animals to survive this cold is a tiny insect.

4 The beagle is a short, strong dog because it was bred to hunt rabbits. It is so short that it is the same size as a rabbit. Thus the beagle can squeeze into a burrow. Being short and strong allows it to turn quickly, just like a rabbit.

5   Miss Terry, the private detective, decided that she was going to be brave, no matter what. If she was outnumbered by the criminals, she would try to outsmart them. If she were captured, she would try to escape. If they threatened her, she would threaten them right back. Those are some of the things she told herself as she heard the criminals coming toward where she was hiding.

6   Dr. Zee claimed he had invented a liquid that would make things disappear. Dr. Zee claimed he had invented a machine that could take people forward or backward in time. Dr. Zee claimed that he was the only scientist with any brains in the whole wide world. Dr. Zee was a very conceited man.

The sentences that tell more about the topic sentence are called supporting sentences. A supporting sentence gives information about the main idea of the paragraph. If a sentence does not tell about the main idea, it is not a supporting sentence and should not be in the paragraph.

EXERCISE 9

Number your answer sheet from 1 to 7. Read each sentence. If it is the topic sentence, write **T** next to the number. If it is a supporting sentence, write **S**. If it does not belong in the paragraph, write **No** next to it.

1.   A man named Stede Bonnet was a wealthy plantation owner.

2.   But he gave it all up to become a pirate.

3. Since many pirates were caught and most were hung, this does not make sense.

4. Blackbeard was a famous pirate.

5. But it made sense to Stede Bonnet.

6. Blackbeard was the most inhuman of the pirates.

7. Stede Bonnet became a pirate because he wanted adventure.

EXERCISE **10**

Number your answer sheet from 1 to 7. Read each sentence. If it is the topic sentence, write **T** next to the number. If it is a supporting sentence, write **S**. If it does not belong in the paragraph, write **No** next to it.

1. There are several fruits that are strictly North American.

2. The cranberry is the best example.

3. That is because it is probably the first fruit the settlers came across in North America.

4. Cranberries go well with sweet things, like oranges.

5. The Indians taught the settlers how to eat cranberries.

6. Another North American fruit is the pawpaw.

7. Cranberries grow in bogs.

EXERCISE **11**

Number your answer sheet from 1 to 6. Read each sentence. If it is the topic sentence, write **T** next to the number. If it is a supporting sentence, write **S**. If it does not belong in the paragraph, write **No** next to it.

1. *Sherlock Holmes* was an early silent film.

2. When talking pictures were invented, even more detective films were made.

10

3. Monster films were also made.

4. So were comedies.

5. Three of the early talking detectives in movies were Philo Vance, Inspector Cockrill, and Sam Spade.

6. Detective movies have been around for a long time.

12

Number your answer sheet from 1 to 9. Read each sentence. If it is the topic sentence, write **T** next to the number. If it is a supporting sentence, write **S**. If it does not belong in the paragraph, write **No** next to it.

1. Because he had once been a gentleman, Stede Bonnet worried about what people thought of him.

2. A man named Dixey Bull was a trader who became a pirate.

3. Most pirates killed the crews of the ships they captured.

4. Stede Bonnet, however, did not want to kill the crews.

5. He did not want people to call him a murderer.

6. So Stede Bonnet captured the crews and dropped them off on islands that were far away.

7. That way, people would not say that Stede Bonnet was a murdering pirate.

8. Another kind pirate was Captain Mission.

9. Captain Mission had been raised as an army officer.

13

Label your answer sheet Exercise 13. Read all the facts below. They are about earthworms. The facts are not in sentences. After you read all the facts, write a topic sentence for a paragraph on earthworms. Then write one supporting sentence for each of the facts. When you have finished, you will have a paragraph that is 8 sentences long.

1. 3,000 different kinds

2. some less than inch long

3. some 10-feet long

4. most brown or red

5. some white or green

6. all live in ground

7. all help improve soil

14

Label your answer sheet Exercise 14. Read the list of names below. These are names of cartoon characters, a professional athlete and a movie. Write a sentence using each of the **names**. At the end of your paragraph, write a topic sentence. When you have finished, you will have a paragraph that is 6 sentences long.

1 Space Jam (movie)

2. Michael Jordan

3. Bugs Bunny

4. Daffy Duck

5. Monstars

All good paragraphs use some sort of transitions. Transitions are words that help show the connection between sentences. They are used at the beginning or in the middle of sentences. Some words that are transitional words are: **and, but, however, because, on the other hand, also, though, if, for example, so, for instance.**

Turn to Exercise 1. Read the second paragraph, the one on farriers. The third sentence begins with the transitional word **and**. The seventh sentence begins with the transitional word **so**. These words help show the connections between the facts or ideas in a paragraph.

15

    Number your answer sheet from 1 to 6. In each group of words, only one is a transitional word. Write the transitional word on your paper.

1.   to, it, but
2.   also, we, the
3.   for example, on, late
4.   she, in, though
5.   which, likely, on the other hand
6.   into, quickly, so

EXERCISE **16**

    Number your answer sheet from 1 to 4. Look at the transitional words listed in the box on page 12. Then answer the questions.

1.   Which transitional words show that a different idea is coming up?
2.   Which transitions show that a similar idea is coming up?
3.   Which transitions tell the reader that something is an example?
4.   Which transitions give reasons?

EXERCISE **17**

    Number your answer sheet from 1 to 16. Read the four paragraphs below. There are a total of sixteen transitional words in the four paragraphs. Write these sixteen words on your paper.

    1   Laughter is good for you. Scientists have discovered that laughing releases more disease-fighting cells in your body. This helps your body to stay healthy. If you're already sick, laughter can help you recover more quickly. So many hospitals now offer comedy channels for their patients to watch.

2   Laughter can relieve stress. For instance, if you are getting ready to take a big test, a joke might help you relax and do better. Laughter can help you get rid of stressful anger also. Next time you get angry, run to a mirror. Look at the funny expression on your face and laugh, because it will make you feel better.

3   Does exercise feel like hard work? Then try laughing instead. Laughter can be great exercise. It uses the same muscles as push-ups. However, laughter is much more fun! Doctors say 20 seconds of laughing can equal the benefits of 3 minutes of hard rowing. So stop sweating and start laughing! It's good for you.

4   Most people laugh at hiccups, but hiccups can be serious if they don't go away. Hiccups that last for days can cause a person to lose weight. They can also exhaust your body. A major league baseball pitcher, for example, had hiccups for nine days and had to be hospitalized.

Another thing that helps show the connection between the main idea and the supporting sentences is repetition. Sometimes one word is repeated, but usually a group of words is repeated at the beginning of a sentence.

Turn to Exercise 1 and read the first paragraph. That paragraph about pirates has six sentences. The third, fourth, and fifth sentences begin with the words "There are pirates in." This repetition helps get across the main idea, that pirates were everywhere.

EXERCISE **18**

Number your answer sheet from 1 to 3. Read each paragraph. Write which word or group of words is repeated in each paragraph to help make the connection between the main idea and the supporting sentences.

1 Dr. Zee claimed he had invented a liquid that would make things disappear. Dr. Zee claimed he had invented a machine that could take people forward or backward in time. Dr. Zee claimed that he was the only scientist with any brains in the whole wide world. Dr. Zee was a very conceited man.

2 People wear masks for many reasons. Halloweeners wear them in order to fool people and get treats. Outlaws wear them so that they won't be recognized. People at parties wear them just for fun. In ancient Greece actors used to wear them to play different parts on the stage. And in ancient China warriors used to wear them in battle to frighten their enemies.

3 There is a fish called the mosquitofish. The fish does not look like a mosquito. It does not buzz like a mosquito. And it does not bite people like a mosquito does. What the mosquito fish does is eat mosquitoes.

EXERCISE 19

Label your answer sheet Exercise 19. Read the following pieces of information about the causes of hiccups. Write a topic sentence for the paragraph. Then write one supporting sentence for each of the facts. End sentences A, B, and D with the words "can cause the hiccups." When you are finished, you will have a paragraph that is five sentences long.

A. 33 different diseases

B. eating spicy foods

C. fright

D. eating or drinking too fast

EXERCISE 20

Label your answer sheet Exercise 20. Read the following information, about Captain Bartholomew Roberts, a pirate. Write one supporting sentence for each of the facts. Help make the paragraph clear by using repetition. Repeat the words "Captain Bartholomew Roberts forbid" at the beginning of the first three sentences. Write a topic sentence at the end of the paragraph. When you have finished. You will have a paragraph that is 5 sentences long.

1. the drinking of alcohol on his ship

2. fighting on Sunday

3. gambling

4. lights had to be out at 8:00 every night

16

Most paragraphs are written in a certain kind of order. If the supporting sentences were all mixed up, the paragraph would be confusing. One kind of order is time order. In time order, the facts or ideas are written about in the order that they happened. Something that happened in 1970 would be talked about before something that happened in 1980. Something that happened at noon would be talked about before something that happened at 5:00 p.m.

Number your answer sheet from 1 to 8. Read the following sentences, which make up a paragraph on detective movies. Write the topic sentence first. Then write the rest of the sentences in the order that they should come in the paragraph.

A. In 1937 Hollywood started to make movies about a Japanese detective, Mr. Moto.

B. The first Mr. Moto film was *Think Fast, Mr. Moto.*

C. At one time, Hollywood made many films about Oriental detectives.

D. In 1915 a silent movie, *The Mission of Mr. Foo*, began the trend.

E. But the first important film with a Chinese detective was *The House Without a Key*, made in 1926.

F. *The House Without a Key* was about the Chinese detective Charlie Chan.

G. And in 1938 the Chinese detective Mr. Wong was introduced.

H. The first movie about Mr. Wong was called *Mr. Wong, Detective.*

17

Another kind of order in paragraphs is direction. Direction can be from top to bottom or from right to left. It could also go from the inside to the outside, or the outside to the inside. If you were writing a paragraph about your room, for example, you could describe it from top to bottom, or from left to right. But you should not jump all around because that would be confusing.

EXERCISE **22**

Number your answer sheet from 1 to 7. Read the following sentences, which make up a paragraph about igloos. Write the topic sentences **first**. Then write the rest of the sentences so that you describe the igloo from the **outside** to the **inside**.

A. The inside of the house is quite warm.
B. All the outside cracks between the blocks are filled with snow so that the igloo is solid.
C. The outside of the house looks like half of a white snowball.
D. The igloo is a round Eskimo house made out of snow.

E. If you look closely, you will see that the snowball is made out of blocks of snow.

F. In fact, the Eskimo must chop a small hole in the center of the ceiling to let out some of the warmth.

G. If the Eskimo did not chop this hole, the house would melt.

You can also give order to paragraphs by size. You can describe something from the littlest to the biggest. Or, you can describe it from the biggest to the littlest. But, do not jump around from middle-sized to big to little.

EXERCISE 23

Number your answer sheet from 1 to 7. Read the sentences about the igloo again. Write the topic sentence **first**. Then write the rest of the sentences so that you describe the igloo from the **inside** to the **outside.**

EXERCISE 24

Number your answer sheet from 1 to 7. Read the sentences, which make up a paragraph about dogs. Write the topic sentence **last**. Then write the rest of the sentences so that you describe the dogs going from the **largest** down to the **smallest.**

A. There are many middle-sized dogs like the French poodle, beagle, and fox terrier.

B. The St. Bernard is also a very large dog, although not as large as the Great Dane.

C. The Pomeranian is a small dog which weighs about six pounds.

D. The Great Dane is the largest of dogs.

E. As you can see, dogs come in all sizes.

F. The world's smallest dog is the Chihuahua.

G. A full grown Chihuahua weighs about two pounds.

EXERCISE 25

Number your answer sheet from 1 to 8. Read the sentences above one more time. Write the topic sentence **last.** Then write the rest of the sentences so that you describe the dogs going from the **smallest** to the **largest.**

One other way to give order to paragraphs is through importance. A paragraph can begin with the most important idea or thing and end with the least important. Or, it can begin with the least important and end with the most important.

26

Number your answer sheet from 1 to 8. Read the sentences, which make up a paragraph about fruit. Write the topic sentence **first**. Then write the letters of the rest of the sentences so that the paragraph talks about the **most important** fruits first, and ends with the **least important.**

A. Other important fruits are the avocado, fig, and breadfruit.

B. Some people eat the avocado, fig, or breadfruit as a major food.

C. That is because bananas, olives, and dates are a major part of some people's diets.

D. In parts of South America, for example, people use the banana just like we use the potato.

E. The least important fruits are those that are snacks or desserts.

F. Just about everybody loves fruit, but some fruits are more important to people than others.

G. These are fruits like oranges, apples, and pears.

H. Bananas, olives, and dates are probably the most important fruits in the world.

27

Number your answer sheet from 1 to 4. Suppose you have to write a paragraph on **"the 50 states of the United States."** Answer each question below.

1. If you had to order your paragraph according to size, how could you do it?

2. If you had to order your paragraph according to time, how could you do it?

3. If you had to order your paragraph according to direction, how could you do it?

4. If you had to order your paragraph according to importance, how could you do it?

Number your answer sheet from 1 to 7. Read each of the paragraphs. On your paper, write the way in which each paragraph is organized. You have four choices: **Time, Size, Direction, Importance**.

1   Most of the commercially important fruits of the world belong to one of two families. The more important of these two, as far as money goes, is the citrus family. Oranges and tangerines are members of the citrus family. So are lemons, limes, and grapefruits. The other family is the rose family. The fruits that are members of the rose family are the apple, peach, apricot, plum, and cherry.

2   At 9:30 a.m., Dr. Zee, the mad scientist, was standing in front of his fellow scientists. As usual, he was telling them that he had just invented something wonderful. This time, he said, he had invented a liquid that would make things disappear. At 9:35, the scientists were laughing at Dr. Zee's claims. At 9:37, Dr. Zee, in a fit of anger, poured the liquid over himself. At 9:38, Dr. Zee had disappeared!

3   From Cairo, the Great Pyramid appears massive at a height of 480 feet. It's as tall as a 40-story building and 175 feet taller than the Statue of Liberty. Its uniform appearance is majestic and awe-inspiring. From the inside, the Great Pyramid is anything but uniform. There are hidden rooms, ramps, bridges, shafts and tunnels. It's one giant maze designed to keep grave robbers from finding the Pharaoh's treasures.

4   There are three kinds of setters raised today. The most famous is the English setter. It is a long-haired white dog with black flecks all over its coat. The one considered the most beautiful is the Irish setter. It has a red coat. The one that fewest people know about is the Gordon setter. It is black with tan markings on its head and chest.

5   The Nile River, unlike most rivers, flows from the south to the north. In southern Egypt, near the city of Aswan, is a granite quarry used by the ancient Egyptians to build the pyramids and tombs of their kings. Following the river north, you will see the Valley of the Kings. Further north you'll see the pyramids near Cairo. And eventually you will reach the city of Alexandria. It is built near the delta where the Nile empties into the Mediterranean Sea.

6   The world's first horses, which lived millions of years ago, were very tiny. They may have weighed 50 pounds at most. They had toes instead of hooves, and they lived in tropical forests. As the world became colder and the tropical forests disappeared, the little horses grew bigger. Soon they became the size of ponies, and they had hooves instead of toes. But the horse did not reach its present size until humans began to raise horses and breed them for size.

7   Tex, Rex, and Lex were brothers who told fortunes. Tex was the biggest of the brothers, and he had a temper as big as his size. When Tex got mad, he would smash his crystal ball and put a hex on whoever made him mad. Rex was almost as big as Tex, but Rex didn't hex people. Rex had poor eyesight and refused to wear glasses. So when Rex looked into his crystal ball, he always told the customers, "I see a cloudy future." Lex was the littlest brother. His customers called him Laughing Lex because he would look into his crystal ball and laugh. That made the customers uncomfortable.

EXERCISE **29**

Label your answer sheet Exercise 29. Write a topic sentence about the 50 states of the United States. Then write a supporting sentence for each of the states below. Order your paragraph according to **size**. You will have 5 sentences in your paragraph.

1. **California**
2. **Rhode Island**
3. **Alaska**
4. **Texas**

EXERCISE **30**

Label your answer sheet Exercise 30. Write a topic sentence about the 50 states of the United States. Then write a supporting sentence for each of the states below. Order your paragraph according to **direction**. You will have six sentences in your paragraph.

1. **Texas**
2. **Maine**
3. **Alaska**
4. **Hawaii**
5. **California**